IMPRESSIONS *of*

SOUTHERN ENGLAND

Produced by AA Publishing

© AA Media Limited 2009

Published by AA Publishing (a trading name of AA Media Limited, whose registered
office is Fanum House, Basing View,
Basingstoke, Hampshire RG21 4EA; registered number 06112600)

ISBN: 978-0-7495-6166-6
A04133

A CIP catalogue record for this book is available from the British Library.

Printed and bound in China by C & C Offset Printing Co. Ltd

Opposite: Looking out across Alum Bay to The Needles from Headon Warren on the Isle of Wight.

IMPRESSIONS *of*

SOUTHERN ENGLAND

Picture Acknowledgements

The Automobile Association would like to thank the following photographers, companies
and picture libraries for their assistance in the preparation of this book.

Abbreviations for the picture credits are as follows: (t) top; (b) bottom; (l) left; (r) right; (c) centre; (AA) AA World Travel Library.

3 AA/S&O Mathews; 5 AA/J Tims; 7 AA/N Hicks; 8 AA/J Miller; 9 AA/N Hicks; 10 AA/D Hall; 11 AA/S Day; 12 AA/N Setchfield; 13 AA/P Baker; 14 AA/A Burton; 15 AA/W Voysey; 16 AA/A Burton; 17 AA/J Miller; 18 AA/S Day; 19 AA/P Kenward; 20 AA/W Voysey; 21 AA/J Miller; 22 AA/P Kenward; 23 AA/S McBride; 24 AA/W Voysey; 25 AA/N Hicks; 26 AA/M Busselle; 27 AA/J Miller; 28 AA/W Voysey; 29 AA/G Edwardes; 30 AA/A Burton; 31 AA/G Edwardes; 32 AA/D Hall; 33 AA/S Day; 34 AA/N Setchfield; 35 AA/J Tims; 36 AA/J Miller; 37 AA/A Burton; 38 AA/S Day; 39 AA/J Miller; 40 AA/P Kenward; 41 AA/N Setchfield; 42 AA/M Busselle; 43 AA/D Forss; 44 AA/S Day; 45 AA/G Edwardes; 46 AA/S McBride; 47 AA/J Miller; 48 AA/C Jones; 49 AA/J Miller; 50 AA/A Burton; 51 AA/S McBride; 52 AA/J Tims; 53 AA/J Tims; 54 AA/N Hicks; 55 AA/N Hicks; 56 AA/D Forss; 57 AA/J Wood; 58 AA/N Hicks; 59 AA/M Jourdan; 60 AA/A Burton; 61 AA/J Miller; 62 AA/W Voysey; 63 AA/A Burton; 64 AA/R Victor; 65 AA/T Woodcock; 66 AA/J Wood; 67 AA/J Wood; 68 AA/J Tims; 69 AA; 70 AA/S&O Mathews; 71 AA/J Miller; 72 AA/N Hicks; 73 AA/J Wood; 74 AA/A Burton; 75 AA/H Williams; 76 AA/A Burton; 77 AA/S&O Mathews; 78 AA/G Edwardes; 79 AA/N Hicks; 80 AA/N Hicks; 81 AA/J Miller; 82 AA/C Jones; 83 AA/R Tenison; 84 AA/F Stephenson; 85 AA/J Wood; 86 AA/N Hicks; 87 AA/N Hicks; 88 AA/R Turpin; 89 AA/C Jones; 90 AA/W Voysey; 91 AA/D Forss; 92 AA/A Burton; 93 AA/N Hicks; 94 AA/W Voysey; 95 AA/J Wood; 96 AA/J Miller; 97 AA/J Miller; 98 AA/M Moody; 99 AA/M Moody; 100 AA/G Edwardes; 101 AA/J Wood; 102 AA/N Hicks; 103 AA/A Burton; 104 AA/N Hicks; 105 AA/A Burton; 106 AA/S Day; 107 AA/G Edwardes; 108 AA/M Jourdan; 109 AA/B Smith; 110 AA/R Rainford; 111 AA/S Day; 112 AA/C Jones; 113 AA/C Jones; 114 AA/A Lawson; 115 AA/S McBride; 116 AA/P Baker; 117 AA/J Miller; 118 AA/J Miller; 119 AA/J Miller; 120 AA/M Busselle; 121 AA/J Miller; 122 AA/G Edwardes; 123 AA/A Burton; 124 AA/J Miller; 125 AA/S McBride; 126 AA/N Hicks; 127 AA/A Lawson; 128 AA/D Hall; 129 AA/N Hicks; 130 AA/J Wood; 131 AA/J Wood; 132 AA/J Miller; 133 AA/J Miller; 134 AA/N Hicks; 135 AA/J Wood; 136 AA/M Busselle; 137 AA/S Day; 138 AA/R Fletcher; 139 AA/A Baker; 140 AA/J Wood; 141 AA/A Burton; 142 R Mort; 143 AA/W Voysey; 144 AA/H Nicks; 145 AA/S Day; 146 AA/J Miller; 147 AA/N Hicks; 148 AA/A Burton; 149 AA/A Burton; 150 AA/G Edwardes; 151 AA/H Nicks; 152 AA/J Wood; 153 AA/M Jourdan; 154 AA/M Moody; 155 AA/J Tims; 156 AA/D Forss; 157 AA/D Hall; 158 AA/J Wood; 159 AA/J Wood.

Every effort has been made to trace the copyright holders, and we apologise in advance for any accidental errors.
We would be happy to apply any corrections in the following edition of this publication.

Opposite: Sunset over the Thames at the Millennium Bridge in Bankside, London.

INTRODUCTION

Think of Southern England and you may conjure up images of overcrowded towns and cities linked by traffic-clogged motorways. Flick through the following pages and you will discover that a rich and varied landscape exists south and west of the M25 and the great capital city of London.

The sprawling metropolis of London pulsates with life: hectic, buzzing and vibrant. There are great historic sights, fascinating museums, exciting markets, and a more genteel side, reflected in its great parks, heaths and elegant squares, and you can escape the hustle and bustle by exploring the Thames by boat.

The Thames Path follows the meandering river west out of the capital through the rolling Berkshire Downs and on into rural Oxfordshire and the gently rising hills of the Cotswolds, noted for its idyllic stone villages nestling in delightful wooded valleys. Much of the route is through a lush countryside of woods and waterside meadows but the river also passes many historic places, including Oxford's dreaming spires and ancient colleges, and Windsor Castle, England's largest inhabited castle.

The south-east corner of the region juts into the English Channel, its marshes, wide beaches and high cliffs are backed by the rolling Sussex downs, the orchards and hop gardens of the Kentish Weald and the colourful heaths and wooded hills of Surrey. The South Downs coast has long been a favoured holiday destination, the salty, sea air luring beach-lovers to a variety of popular resorts, from the eccentric fun of Brighton to traditional favourites such as Worthing and Eastbourne, and the historic charm of Rye and Chichester.

The breezy South Downs represents some of the finest walking in southern England, the 90-mile South Downs Way runs like a thread across the ridge of hills, taking you west into Hampshire. Here, nature-lovers can escape to the woods and heaths of the New Forest, and you an explore the great historic city of Winchester, and follow peaceful towpaths and trails beside the crystal-clear chalk streams. Across The Solent lies the Isle of Wight, a holiday island with a family atmosphere and a timeless, old fashioned appeal, ringed by wide beaches and chalk cliffs. From the busy resort of Bournemouth, the Avon Valley leads to the peace of the Wiltshire Downs. Wiltshire evokes images of ancient stone circles, white chalk horses carved into hillsides, crop circles, the forbidden, empty landscape of Salisbury Plain, and miles of uninterrupted views deep into Dorset and Somerset.

Beyond lies the West Country, a dwindling peninsula reaching out in to the Atlantic, inspiring a real sense of Island Britain. It's an area of great natural beauty, embracing the lush pastures and the high, wild moorland of Devon, Cornwall's rugged cliffs, the serene and rolling landscape of Dorset, and the flatness and huge skies of the Somerset Levels. It's a rich rural land, famed for its landscape of rolling hills and steep river valleys, and its warm climate and magnificent coastline make it Britain's most popular holiday destination.

Opposite: Rose-covered cottage wall in Bossington, Exmoor National Park, Somerset.

View across Hastings Old Town to East Hill and the sea.

Anglers fishing in Porlock Bay, as seen from Hurlstone Point near Porlock, Exmoor National Park, Somerset.

Cotswold stone cottage and laburnham tree in Chedworth, Gloucestershire.
Opposite: The River Colne meanders through grassy meadows near Cassey Compton, Gloucestershire.

Shoreditch street art by Banksy, a Bristol-based graffiti artist, London.

Attractive shop front in Church Street, Dunster, Exmoor National Park, Somerset.

Rhododendrons on the Rhinefield Ornamental Drive near Brockenhurst, New Forest.

Quaint riverside cottages in the wooded Barle Valley at Dulverton, Exmoor National Park, Somerset.

Sunrise over 'Day Dawn' houseboat in Bembridge Harbour, Isle of Wight.

Union Jack flaps in the sea breeze outside The Grand Hotel, Brighton, East Sussex.

Sunlight illuminates the ornate, 14th-century fan-vaulted cloister ceilings at Gloucester Cathedral, Gloucestershire.

Gilt wrought-iron work on Kensington Palace gates, London.

Wild mushrooms and autumn leaves in the New Forest National Park, Hampshire.

Cyclists pedalling the South Downs Way at dusk on the Fulking escarpment, near Devil's Dyke, East Sussex.

Floodlit detail on the Albert Bridge, spanning the River Thames in London.
The structure is floodlit at night, rows of lights attached to the suspension wires.

The Needles and The Solent from chalk cliffs at Scratchell's Bay, Isle of Wight.

Red deer in the New Forest National Park, Hampshire.
Opposite: Flowering hawthorn near Dartmeet, Dartmoor National Park, Devon.

Looking along the beach and promenade from the pier at Eastbourne, East Sussex.

Lines of deckchairs on the promenade at Eastbourne, East Sussex.

View across the River Thames to the Tower of London.

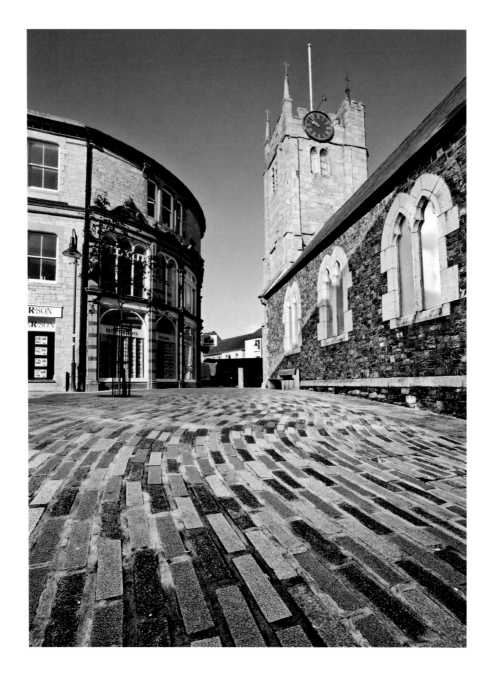

A town centre scene in Okehampton, Devon.

Belted Galloway cows graze contentedly on Beaulieu Heath, New Forest National Park, Hampshire.
Opposite: Remains of Wheal Betsy Tin Mine near Tavistock, Dartmoor National Park, Devon.

Broadway Tower crowns the second highest point in the Cotswolds.

A pastoral scene around Snowshill in the Cotswolds.

The dome of St Paul's Cathedral viewed through the Millennium Bridge at Bankside, London.

Jogger on the Thames Path passing Henley Temple on Temple Island at Henley, Oxfordshire.

*The meandering Cuckmere river and the South Downs from the Seven Sisters Country Park
near Alfriston, East Sussex.*

A grey squirrel admires thatched Cole Cottage in the New Forest National Park, Hampshire.

A quintessential thatched Cotswold stone cottage in Chipping Campden, Oxfordshire.

A patchwork quilt of colourful fields brighten up the South Downs near Brighton, East Sussex.

Richard Rogers' impressive Lloyds Building in London.

South Bank lion statue at Westminster Bridge, London.

Footpath leading to the Wilmington Long Man and the South Downs near Alfriston, East Sussex.
Opposite: Looking across Freshwater Bay to Tennyson Down from thrift-covered cliffs near Freshwater, Isle of Wight.

Gabled 17th-century dovecote nestling in a peaceful valley near Naunton, Gloucestershire.

St Peter's Church clock, Buckland in the Moor, Dartmoor National Park, Devon.

Sunset across Alum Bay on the Isle of Wight.

Low tide at Bexhill seafront, East Sussex.

Beachcombing at Bexhill, East Sussex.
Opposite: The Valley of the Rocks, Exmoor National Park, Devon.

A groyne zig-zigs down Calshot beach, with distant views of the Isle of Wight.

Sailing boats on the Solent at Cowes harbour, Isle of Wight.

View across the River Thames to All Saints Church at Marlow, Buckinghamshire.

Time to reflect – on the River Wey at Guildford, Surrey.

The River Dart flows through the verdant Dart Valley Nature Reserve at New Bridge, Dartmoor National Park, Devon.
Opposite: Wild flowers in the Valley of the Rocks, Exmoor National Park, Devon.

Osborne House, the Italianate summer home designed by Prince Albert for Queen Victoria, at East Cowes, Isle of Wight.

Wrought-iron bench, Trelissick Gardens, near Truro, Cornwall.

Buckfast Abbey, Buckfastleigh, Dartmoor National Park, Devon.

Deckchairs billow in the summer breeze in Hyde Park, London.

Unusual clock tower on Ventnor esplanade, Isle of Wight.

View of Lewes from the castle, East Sussex.

Butterfly on hedgerow flowers in Adgestone Vineyard, Isle of Wight.
Opposite: Autumnal scene in Bolderwood Forest, New Forest National Park, Hampshire.

Household Cavalry Guard on parade in London.

Detail of the Gothic façade of St Pancras Station, London.

Pebbles on Millook beach, near Crackington Haven, Cornwall.

Opposite: Stunning view across Porthcurno Beach, near Land's End, Cornwall.

The London Eye and County Hall on the south bank of the River Thames, London.

The 18th-century chalk figure of the Long Man of Wilmington, etched into the South Downs near Alfriston, East Sussex.

The ornate splendour of the Royal Pavilion in Brighton, East Sussex.
Opposite: Looking out to sea from the Palace Pier at Brighton, East Sussex.

A panoramic view across rolling fields towards Dartmoor from Marldon, Devon.

An orange tree flourishes in the warm Temperate Biome at the Eden Project, near St Austell, Cornwall.

Reedmace seed heads at Cannop Ponds, Forest of Dean, Gloucestershire.
Opposite: Sunrise over sand dunes at Mudeford, Dorset.

Georgian brick cottages line the timeless street leading to the Beaulieu River at Buckler's Hard,

New Forest National Park.

'Fields of Gold', near Alfriston, East Sussex.

St Peter's Church in Buckland in the Moor, Dartmoor National Park, Devon.

A rocky outcrop along the sea cliff in the Valley of the Rocks, near Lynton, Exmoor National Park, Devon.

Ruined chapel window at Okehampton Castle, Dartmoor National Park, Devon.

Looking along the South Downs escarpment from Devil's Dyke, near Brighton, East Sussex.

A pretty harbour scene at Lynmouth, Exmoor National Park, Devon.

Opposite: A coast path view across rugged cliffs to Lizard Point on the south Cornish coast.

Ancient stone cottages tumble down the hill in the postcard-pretty Cotswold village of Snowshill, Gloucestershire.

Highland cattle at Colliford Lake, Bodmin Moor, Cornwall.

A view up the River Dart and across to Dartmouth from Kingswear, Devon.
Oppoite: Smeaton's Tower, Britain's first lighthouse, on Plymouth Hoe, Devon.

The Oxo Tower, a former power station housing shops, restaurants and an exhibition space, beside the Thames at Southwark, London.

A view across the River Thames to the City of London and the striking Gherkin Building.

Wild ponies on heathland in the New Forest National Park, Hampshire.
Opposite: Sunset over Compton Bay, Isle of Wight.

A water lily-covered pond at Furzey Gardens, near Lyndhurst, New Forest National Park.

On the ramparts of Totnes Castle, Totnes, Devon.

Relaxing on the flowering banks of the Cuckmere River at Cuckmere Haven, East Sussex.

The Tate Gallery in St Ives exhibits the very best of Cornish contemporary art.

The giant chalk cliffs tower over the lighthouse at Beachy Head, East Sussex.

Colourful houses in the North Laine area of Brighton, East Sussex.

View over rolling downland from Butser Hill, near Petersfield, Hampshire.

The 13th-century thatched Fulling Mill straddles the River Itchen at Alresford, Hampshire.

The ancient clapper bridge over the River Dart near Postbridge, Dartmoor National Park, Devon.

Sculptural stone forms of Showery Tor on Bodmin Moor, Cornwall.

An idyllic waterfall scene at Watersmeet, near Lynmouth, Exmoor National Park, Devon.

Fallow deer graze on the plains near Stoney Cross, New Forest National Park, Hampshire.

Rock climbers scale Haytor, Dartmoor National Park, Devon.
Opposite: Heather and bracken carpet rolling heathland at Rockford Common, New Forest National Park, Hampshire.

The Cotswold Way footpath leads to Painswick Beacon and glorious views across rolling Cotswold countryside.

Bowerman's Nose on Hayne Down near Manaton, Dartmoor National Park, Devon.

Norman Foster designed the Great Court canopy in London's British Museum.

Number Ten Downing Street, the home of Britain's Prime Minister.

The crystal clear waters of the River Coln at Bibury, Gloucestershire.

Bright crimson poppies burst out of the Long Border in Snowshill Manor Gardens, Gloucestershire.

Gorse and heather add a splash of colour to the landscape at Haytor, Dartmoor National Park, Devon.

The dramatic rocky crag of Castle Rock in the Valley of the Rocks, near Lynton, Exmoor National Park, Devon.

The baroque grandeur of Blenheim Palace glows at sunset, Woodstock, Oxfordshire.

The striking glass structure of City Hall, home to the Mayor of London, stands on the south bank near Tower Bridge.

Thatched cottages border the green in the hamlet of Swan Green near Lyndhurst,
New Forest National Park, Hampshire.

The meandering Cuckmere River snakes a path through the meadows in the Seven Sisters Country Park near Alfriston, East Sussex.

Sunset over a floodlit Brighton Pier, East Sussex.

A lazy sunny day on Brighton beach, East Sussex.

The South Downs escarpment on a summer's day near Alfriston, East Sussex.

Birds following a furrowing tractor on the South Downs in Sussex.

Ponies seek shade in the New Forest National Park, Hampshire.
Opposite: Sunset at Vixen Tor, south of Merrivale, Dartmoor National Park, Devon.

Walkers on the South Downs Way above the Seven Sisters, East Sussex.

Dusk over The Needles and chalk cliffs on the Isle of Wight.

A pebble beach and wooded coastline near Porlock, Exmoor National Park, Somerset.

A summer view of Robin Hill from Tivington, Exmoor National Park, Somerset.

The splendid gardens at Berkeley Castle, Gloucestershire.

Cairn on the summit of Dunkery Beacon, Exmoor National Park, Somerset.

Following the coast path to Porth Moina, near Zennor, Cornwall.

Keep Out – scarecrow doll guarding a gate at Colliford Lake, Cornwall.

Elegant terrace houses in Regency Square, Brighton, East Sussex.

Fishing at low tide from Eastbourne beach, East Sussex.

Detail of the supporting buttresses on the ancient bridge over the River Barle at Tarr Steps, near Dulverton, Exmoor National Park.
Opposite: Pastoral scene looking across fields to the sea at Zennor, near Land's End, Cornwall.

Path leading to the South Downs near Alfriston, East Sussex.

The ruins of 13th-century Hailes Abbey, near Winchcombe, Gloucestershire.

Mist and shafts of sunlight in autumnal oak and beech woodland, off the A35 near Bank, New Forest National Park, Hampshire.

A beautiful, ivy-clad, Cotswold stone cottage in Minchinhampton, Gloucestershire.

Island Bridge spans the crashing waves on Towan Beach, Newquay, Cornwall.

The Giant Sequoias (Wellingtonias) on the Rhinefield Ornamental Drive, near Brockenhurst, New Forest National Park.

Ornamental lamp posts line the Embankment beside the River Thames, London.

A steamer in St Katherine's Dock at London Docklands.

The rushing waters of Becky Falls, near Manaton, Dartmoor National Park, Devon.

The impressive 19th-century Bliss Tweed Mill, since converted into apartments, in Chipping Norton, Oxfordshire.

Lichens and English Stonecrop cling to an old stone wall at Porlock Weir, Exmoor National Park, Somerset.
Opposite: Early morning view looking west along the South Downs from Devil's Dyke, East Sussex.

The imposing gatehouse entrance to Carisbrooke Castle, Isle of Wight.

Walkers caught in a burst of sunlight through the trees at Bolderwood, New Forest National Park, Hampshire.

The remains of a Bronze Age settlement at Grimspound, Dartmoor National Park, Devon.

Jagged cliffs at Heddon's Mouth Cove, Exmoor National Park, Devon.

The unusual, whitewashed Huers hut at Newquay, Cornwall.

Opposite: Stunning panoramic view of the sweeping cove and chalk cliffs at Durdle Door, Dorset.

The River Itchen and the 13th-century thatched Fulling Mill in Alresford, Hampshire.

Wooden walkway over the River Thames towards Marsh Lock from Henley, Oxfordshire.

A path through beech woodland near Burley, New Forest National Park, Hampshire.

Wild garlic growing near Malmesbury, Wiltshire.

Rev Hawker's Hut on the coast path at Morwenstow, Cornwall.
Opposite: Cliff climbing at Port Moina, near Land's End, Cornwall.

INDEX

Adgestone Vineyard 63
Alfriston 42, 77, 120, 136
Alresford 99, 154
Alum Bay 46

Barle Valley, Devon 15
Beachy Head 96
Beaulieu Heath 30
Becky Falls 144
Bembridge 16
Berkley Castle 128
Bexhill 47, 49
Bibury 110
Blenheim Palace 114
Bliss Tweed Mill 145
Bodmin Moor 85, 131
Bolderwood 63, 149
Bossington 6
Bowerman's Nose 107
Brighton 17, 39, 71, 97, 118, 119, 132
British Museum 108
Broadway Tower 32
Brockenhurst 14
Buckfast Abbey 58
Buckland in the Moor 45, 78
Buckler's Hard 76
Burley 156
Butser Hill 98

Cannop ponds 75
Carisbrooke Castle 148
Cassey Compton 10
Chedworth 10
Chipping Campden 38
Chipping Norton 145
City Hall, London 115
Compton Bay 90
Cotswold Way 106
County Hall, London 68
Cowes, Isle of Wight 51

Cuckmere Haven 94
Cukmere River 36, 117

Dartmoor 24, 29, 30, 45, 54, 58, 72, 78,
    80, 100, 104, 107, 112, 123, 144, 150
Dartmouth 87
Dart Valley 54
Devil's Dyke 21, 81, 147
Downing Street, London 109
Dulverton 15, 134
Dunkery Beacon 129
Dunster 13
Durdle Door 152

Eastbourne 26, 27, 133
Eden Project, Cornwall 73
Embankment, London 142
Exmoor 6, 9, 13, 15, 49, 55, 79, 82, 102,
    113, 126, 127, 129, 134, 147, 151

Freshwater Bay 42
Fulking Escarpment 21
Furzey Gardens, New Forest 92

Gherkin Building, London 89
Gloucester Cathedral 18
Guildford 53

Hailes Abbey
Hastings 8
Haytor 104, 112
Heddon's Mouth 151
Henley 35, 155
Hurlsone Point 9
Hyde Park, London 59

Isle of Wight 23, 46, 50, 51, 56, 60,
    90, 125

Kensington Palace, London 19

Land's End 66, 130, 134, 158
Lewes 61
Lizard Point 82
Lloyds Building, London 40
London 4, 12, 19, 34, 40, 41, 59, 65, 68,
    88, 109, 142, 143
London Eye 68
Long Man of Wilmington 69
Lyndhurst 116
Lynmouth 82, 102

Malmesbury 157
Mardon 72
Marlow 52
Marsh Lock, Henley 155
Millennium Bridge, London 4, 34
Millook 66
Morwenstow 158
Mudeford 75

Naunton 44
Needles, The 23, 125
New Forest 14, 20, 24, 30, 37, 63, 76,
    90, 92, 104, 116, 123, 138, 141, 149,
    156
Newquay 140, 152

Okehampton 29, 80
Oxo Tower, London
Osborne House, Isle of Wight 56

Painswick Beacon 106
Palace Pier, Brighton 71
Plymouth 87
Porlock 9
Porthcurno Beach, Cornwall 66
Porth Moina, Cornwall 130, 158
Postbridge 100

Rhinefield Ornamental Drive 14, 141
River Barle 15, 134
River Coln 110
River Dart 87
Robin Hill 127
Rockford Common 104
Rough Tor 101
Royal Pavilion, Brighton 71

St Katherine's Dock, London 143
St Pancras Station, London 65
St Paul's Cathedral, London 34
Seven Sisters 124
Smeaton's Tower, Plymouth 87
Snowshill 33, 84, 111
South Bank, London 41
South Downs 39, 42, 69, 81, 120, 121,
    136
Stoney Cross 103

Tarr Steps 134
Tate St Ives 95
Temple Island, Henley 35
Totnes 93
Tower of London 28
Trelissick Gardens, Cornwall 57

Valley of the Rocks 49, 55, 79, 113
Ventnor, Isle of Wight 60
Vixen Tor 123

Watersmeet 102
Wheal Betsy Tin Mine 30
Woodstock 114

Zennor 134